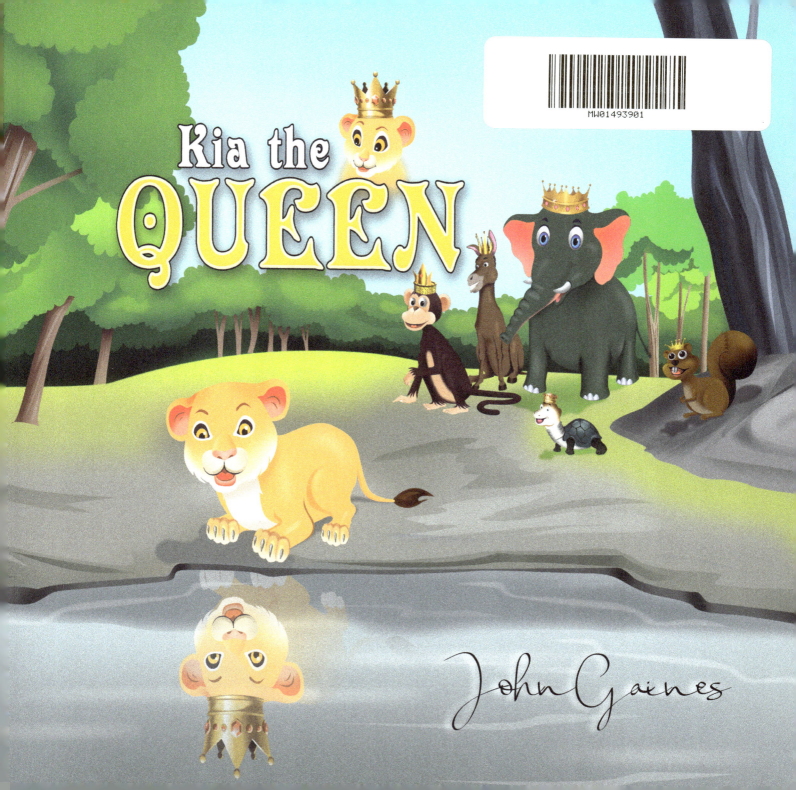

Kia the QUEEN

John Gaines

KIA THE QUEEN

This book is written to provide information and motivation to readers. Its purpose is not to render any type of psychological, legal, or professional advice of any kind. The content is the sole opinion and expression of the author, and not necessarily that of the publisher.

Printed in the United States of America.

ISBN   978-1-949746-30-3   (Paperback)
ISBN   978-1-949746-31-0   (Digital)

Lettra Press books may be ordered through booksellers or by contacting:

Lettra Press LLC
18229 E 52nd Ave.
Denver City, CO 80249
1 303 586 1431 | info@lettrapress.com
www.lettrapress.com

About the Author

John Gaines aka John "PUSH" Gaines is a former at-risk Kinship Care kid turned youth advocate, motivational speaker, entrepreneur, and author.

Through his organization, The PUSH for Dreams Leadership Academy, John has spoken at universities, nonprofit organizations, youth conferences, NBA skill camps, churches, and schools. He has worked with groups of parents, educators, coaches & mental health professionals.

John attended East Central University where he graduated Outstanding Student in Business and won a football championship as captain of the football team.

Also, he graduated from Liberty University with a Master degree in Business Leadership. John currently lives in Tacoma, Washington with his wife, Emily, daughter Anorah and his dog, Lola.

The purpose of this book is to help young readers realize they have value, they are important, and it is okay to believe in themselves.

This book will give all young readers the hope they need to be great despite the adversity or obstacles they will face in life.

To my beautiful wife, Emily and my precious daughter Anorah. Your support means the world to me.

To my brother and sister-in-law, Donyelle and V. Rebecca Frazier. With your help, I found the King within.

To my first-grade teacher Alisa Keolker. Thank you for believing in me.

Kia, the lion cub, was born to be a Queen, but it took her a long time to realize it because of the challenges she faced.

One of the challenges Kia faced was that her parents were lost forever while they were on a dangerous hunt for food in the Safari.

Luckily for Kia, she had an older brother, named Prince Jaja. He was one year away from protecting the whole Safari and being a King for all of the animals in the Safari.

He was not quite ready to raise a young lion cub, but he stepped up to raise Kia along with his Princess, named Amina.

Kia faced a few challenges as a cub. She didn't live with her parents like the other animals in the Safari, she talked funny, and she could not read as well as the other animals in her class.

Even though Kia had a brother and sister-in-law who cared for her, she missed and thought about her parents every day.

When she began school, she couldn't read well, and she pronounced words differently than the other animals in her class.

Many of the animals in her class made fun of her because of her differences.

Kia's brother, Prince Jaja would sit with her every day after school and tutor her. He helped her learn how to read because he did not want animals in her class to make fun of her.

One day at school, Kia's teacher, Ms. C taught the class about the importance of having a dream for themselves and the importance of believing in themselves.

That day in class Kia told Ms. C she wanted to be a Queen and Ms. C looked at Kia with great joy and said, "I believe in you!"

Ms. C told Kia she believed in her because she knew all animals that are born would eventually become a Queen or a King despite the challenges they faced in their life.

In that very moment, Kia began to believe in herself. She wanted to be a Queen more than anything. She believed in herself so much, she would dream of being a Queen every night.

For Kia to become who she was created to be, a Queen, she had to think it, believe it and then achieve it. For her to reach it, she had to work hard every day and realize she had great value even though other animals made fun of her.

Kia continued to work on her reading and speech because she hoped to succeed. Every day on her way to school she would look at herself in the water and yell out loud, "I am a QUEEN!" And because of that small action, Kia began to see herself as a Queen.

Kia followed the same routine every day until she made it all the way to Animal Promotion School.
Animal Promotion School is the school Kia had to pass before she could become an official Queen.
It was tough, but Kia not only moved on, but she happened to be one of the best cubs ever to pass Animal Promotion School.

After Kia's promotion, she went back to the Safari to inspire and encourage all animals to believe in themselves. She would declare, "I believe in you! You have value! You are a King! You are a Queen!"

Kings and Queens are born every day, but for a King or a Queen to be who they were created to be, they must first believe in themselves and realize they have value.

Your positive thoughts will lead to positive actions, and your positive actions will lead to your purpose to be a King or a Queen.

Who you are created to be has nothing to do with how others see you, but it has everything to do with how you see yourself.

Always remember today and each day, Kia believes in you and you are great, no matter the challenges you face.

You have value, no matter the bad things others say or do, and you are a Queen or a King because that is who you were born to be!

Kia the QUEEN

CPSIA information can be obtained
at www.ICGtesting.com
Printed in the USA
LVHW072158191020
669239LV00026B/2547